# I REALLY LIKE LOVERS OF POETRY

Grzegorz Wróblewski

Translated from the Polish by
Grzegorz Wróblewski &
Marcus Silcock Slease

Červená Barva Press
Somerville, Massachusetts

Červená Barva Press
P.O. Box 440357
W. Somerville, MA 02144

www.cervenabarvapress.com

Bookstore: www.thelostbookshelf.com

Production: Allison O'Keefe

Cover art: "50 x 50 The Boys from Amager II" by Grzegorz Wroblewski

ISBN: 978-1-950063-93-2

# CONTENTS

# I REALLY LIKE
# LOVERS OF
# POETRY

# ISOLATION

*I want to finally be a free human being,*
says the rebellious writer.

*How?* I ask him.

*I'm going to steal lemons from the store*
*and they'll put me in jail,*
he explains the advanced
plan.

People can't fly like seagulls.

So they have to sit
in isolation.

# EROTIC LITERATURE

*I have an excellent idea for the title of the next book,*
our friend, the famous playwright,
suddenly sobered up.

*It will be like this: A RELIGIOUS PELICAN,*
*WHO WOKE UP UNEXPECTEDLY IN THE BODY*
*OF A LEECH, AND STARTED WRITING EROTIC*
*LITERATURE FOR THE INHABITANTS*
*OF THE MINISTERED ESTATE.*

*A bit long!* John praised him.

*Long but brilliant,* the playwright began to get
pissed off.

*And what will it even be about?* I asked him.

*It will become clear in the process of creation,*
he replied and opened a new bottle of cider.

# GIRAFFE

If I publicly announced that a giraffe has two heads,
they would immediately comment that I was drunk.
Or that I am a thief or a spy from Jupiter.
In the end, they'd put me in jail.

If, on the other hand, I were to say that a giraffe has
one head, like humans, there would be protests
that I do not believe in God and that I am a follower
of Darwin's theory of evolution.
I would be advised psychotherapy, and in the end
they would put me in prison anyway.

That's why I don't talk about giraffes.
I don't know how many heads a single giraffe has.
But silence is also dangerous.
So my future is very much in doubt.

# I WOULD LIKE TO WAKE UP

Some people do not like wolves
and say that wolves attack children
who come home with heavy schoolbags.

Other people love pigs while eating pig
meat every day. I would like to wake up someday
among people who respect both
wolves and pigs.

In the world of dwarves who eat nuts
and cinnamon-spiced cabbage.

# 9 SLOGANS

1. I didn't want to do it.
2. That's not what I meant.
3. I wasn't myself when I did this.
4. I didn't mean to hurt you.
5. Something tempted me.
6. I am extremely sorry that this happened.
7. It will never happen again.
8. They put something in my glass.
9. We'll be happy together again.

# I REALLY LIKE LOVERS OF POETRY

I really like lovers of poetry. I have a faithful
friend who is always interested in my new
books.

When I hand her the next edition, she asks me
to read a few selected works from it.
And then she asks like this:
*And what do you get out of it?*

And I answer her with a question:
*In what sense?*

Then she explains:
*In an economic sense.*

Then there is a two-minute silence.

And after a while we are already talking
about problems with nature conservation.

And so we have been together since time
immemorial.
I really like lovers of poetry.

# SOMETHING

Surely something can be done.
But what specifically?
This is not known.


But there is still something
that can be done.
This is a popular dilemma.


It appears even when we perform
our dream activities.

## LISTEN...

Listen to the silence of heaven.
You won't understand any of it.

But at least you'll be closer
to the silent clouds.

Closer to where you got here
by a mistake.

# ARTIFICAL INTELLIGENCE

Because of her,
they lengthen people's feet.

But there is a big benefit!

It will be easier for us to tread
across flat earth.

# WRITING POEMS

Writing poems is the same
as creating paintings. You paint words

and note the inner landscapes.
And then people spit on both.

# CHILDREN

Children are people,
not rubber rabbits.

# LOTTERY

You have to be a real idiot to win the lottery.
What do you need to do? Just dial the numbers:
1-2-3-4-5-6-7. Then lie down in the coffin and wait.
Oh, put $500 into my account
for giving you this great advice.

# SINGING BIRDS

We are waiting for spring and sun.
Then the singing birds come.


And then we dream of autumn peace.
We like snow, but only in moderate


amounts. And again we are waiting
for the singing birds.

# TRUTH

Everyone is looking for the truth.
The only truth is the rumbling
of our stomachs.

# WITNESSES

They are loved by everyone.
Witnesses who did not
see or hear anything.

# MY EX-WIFE'S GRANDFATHER

He lived to a ripe old age,
smoked unfiltered cigarettes,

and never read a single book.
But he had the look of Socrates.

# SIMPLE PEOPLE

Simple people can
communicate
well with everyone.


They don't use too many juicy,
bland words,
and have a better life than


those who, when buying apples,
say: *I'll have two apples,
the ones the colour of lemon carrot
with a hint of green,
or rather brown.*


There will still be a worm
in an apple,
no matter how we describe it.

# BEAUTIFUL

Poetry must be beautiful,
with beautiful words and beautiful
symbols.
Even death in poems must be dignified,
solemn and beautiful.
Worms in a beautiful coffin
must also be beautiful.
Best dressed in beautiful robes
with makeup on their glossy mouths.
A priest must be beautiful,
even when he is a hundred
years old.
Everything has to be beautiful.
Life and death are beautiful.

# UNIVERSE

I calmly chew onions like a cow eats grass.
Around war and plague...
And someone is drilling a hole in the wall in the middle
of the night.

# CITIES CAN BE AS BEAUTIFUL AS FORESTS

Cities can be as beautiful as forests & forests can be as beautiful
as cities.
Everything can be favorable to us. But it doesn't always work out
that way.

# AQUARIUM

Aquarium fish are great because they don't have violent arguments with us.

You just need
to feed them.

# A FRIEND

He keeps telling us that
a meteor wiped out the dinosaurs.

And that he used to weigh 200 kilos,
but thanks to his diet,

he weighs 100, but he's still afraid
of weighing 200 again.

Dinosaurs all the time,
200 kilos, 100 kilos.

We are afraid to eat anything
in front of him.

# FLOWERS

We're talking about someone being stupid.
Then he's smart.
(He suddenly became smart!)


Maybe because he lent us
a hundred dollars
or gave us flowers he stole from the cemetery?


Instead of quietly watching the waves
of the sea,
we wonder who is wise or who is stupid.

# SHINING SKYCRAPERS

Shining
skyscrapers
can't

free
themselves
from

sad
eagles,
aimlessly

soaring
above
the anthill
of mad,

lonely
human
hearts.

# GREGORY

Parents decide everything. If they called me Beelzebub,
I'd have problems in school and kids would throw stones
at me.

If my name was Jesus, cheese sandwiches would be stolen
from my backpack with a smile.

Fortunately, I was named
neutrally - Gregory.
And no one paid any attention to me.

The girls didn't put their pink underpants on my head.

I had a boring childhood.

# COUNTRY POETRY

Which is better,
hay or ham?
Hay for some,
ham for others.

# DREAMER

I would like to write a poem about beautiful
flowers.
A poem about yellow petals that smell like
honey.
And then give it to the girl next door who has ignored me


for years. But what if I write it? I'll just look like
an idiot.
She would prefer a poem about racing cars. And most of all,
instead of a poem, she would like me to finally
grab her ass.


But I can't do that.
Because I am a sensitive poet and a dreamer.

# CORAL REEFS

Remember exactly your name. Especially when diving among coral reefs.

At the right moment, you will give your personal information to a hungry shark.

He will definitely be interested in them.

# NOTHING

I wandered the world for a long time
with a black blindfold over my eyes.


I felt the desert wind, the chill of many seas
and the breath of beings rubbing against me.


Finally, one day, after many years,
I took off the blindfold.


Then I saw clearly the destination of my journey:
NOTHING, silent and devoid of any smell.

# MY COUSINS

My cousins wanted me to become a hunter and bring them
deer horns
as gifts.


It's interesting, none of them have ever been
to a shooting range.


One of them drank himself to death at a young age,
and the other graduated from medical school and is now
repairing people's hearts.


I became an observer of sea waves and algae,
a hunter of sunbeams on Danish stone and silent
islands...


I don't have any display cases with butterflies and deer antlers
on the wall.

# OLD TRAVELER

What do you do on sleepless nights, always awake,
old traveler?

I stare at my own shadow and have long chats with it.

What are you talking about? Don't you get angry with the silver
all-knowing moon?

We tell each other about beautiful dreams, full of underwater,
shining creatures that came to us from the land of darkness.

The living and the shadows need closeness. The moon is just
listening.

The moon is just listening.

# INNER GHOST

One night I heard a whisper: Write a poem about me.
After all, you don't exist, it's just my imagination
- I was surprised and wiped the icy sweat
from my forehead.


Whatever you write about me,
I will be with you forever,
you will save me in yourself. I am your only faithful
companion & I want nothing more.


So I wrote the above words. And my inner ghost
never spoke to me again. I didn't ask what I would get out of it
and I didn't find out
why I should actually save him forever.

# SAHARA

I once came across
a settlement in the Sahara desert
where several poor families stayed.


Their camels rested in a tent with holes in it.


We spoke different languages.
They did not understand me, but smiled
without words.


Now, after many years, as the images of the past are slowly
blurring in my mind, I can clearly see the endless ocean
of sand and their big eyes piercing me.


Something connected us forever.

# GREAT FATHER

You will never understand me, Son.
Now,
when you walk down a colorful

street in Copenhagen, you see two dealers
and a huge balloon-like rat.
Enjoy this view!

You will never understand me, Son.
Admire the ladies who put lace panties
in their bags.

Enjoy your life while you can.

# ARMAGEDDON DAYS

There was nothing unusual about it.

Children played in the squares,
and alcoholics slowly drank beer
on the benches.

The sun suddenly changed its color.

The policeman fired
a bullet,
but it hit the nearby trees.

And the world ceased to exist.

# CONVERSATIONS WITH THE PROPHETS

I'm looking for happiness, could you
advise me on how to find it?

And what is happiness for you?

That's what I don't know, I'm tracking
happiness to no avail.

Once you find it, come to me again.

Then I won't need you anymore.

You have it within you, but you must first
see the man with the bird's head
on the solar orb.

It's too complicated.

Happiness is not a watermelon thrown
in the trash.

# ACKNOWLEDGMENTS

Thanks to the editors of the following journals in which some of these poems first appeared:

*Jacket2*: Giraffe
*Eunoia Review*: Listen..., Singing Birds, Witnesses
*Sahitya Post*: 9 Slogans, Artifical Intelligence, Writing Poems,
            Children, Lottery, Truth
*Spill Words*: I Really Like Lovers of Poetry
*Synchronized Chaos*: Great Father, Armageddon Days,
            Conversations with the Prophets
*Himalaya Diary*: Beautiful, I would like to wake up, Something
*Streetcake Magazine*: Isolation

# ABOUT THE AUTHOR

Grzegorz Wróblewski was born in 1962 in Gdańsk and grew up in Warsaw. Since 1985 he has been living in Copenhagen. English translations of his work are available in *Our Flying Objects* (trans. Joel Leonard Katz, Rod Mengham, Malcolm Sinclair, Adam Zdrodowski, Equipage, 2007), *A Marzipan Factory* (trans. Adam Zdrodowski, Otoliths, 2010), *Kopenhaga* (trans. Piotr Gwiazda, Zephyr Press, 2013), *Let's Go Back to the Mainland* (trans. Agnieszka Pokojska, Červená Barva Press, 2014), *Zero Visibility* (trans. Piotr Gwiazda, Phoneme Media, 2017), *Dear Beloved Humans* (trans. Piotr Gwiazda, Lavender/Dialogos Books, 2023) Asemic writing book *Shanty Town* (Post-Asemic Press, 2022).

# ABOUT THE TRANSLATOR

Marcus Silcock Slease is a (mostly) surreal-absurd writer from Portadown, N. Ireland. He is the author of *Puppy* (Beir Bua Press), *Never Mind the Beasts* (Dostoyevsky Wannabe), *The Green Monk* (Boiler House Press), and *Play Yr Kardz Right* (Dostoyevsky Wannabe), among others. His poetry has been translated into Polish and Danish and has appeared or is forthcoming in various magazines and anthologies, including: *Tin House, Poetry, The Lincoln Review, Bath Magg, New World Writing, Tupelo Quarterly*, and in the *Best British Poetry* series. He lives in Sitges, Spain. Find out more at: Never Mind the Beasts (www.nevermindthebeasts.com)

9 781950 063932